The People's History

Around Gateshead

by

John Carlson and Joyce Carlson

A view of modern day Gateshead showing the great changes that have been made around the banks of the Tyne.

Previous page: A group of CWS Pelaw workers during a lunch break outside the factory, *circa* 1951 – Ken Graham, Evelyn Stoves, Maureen Sinclair and Joyce Wilkinson.

Copyright John Carlson and Joyce Carlson 2005

First published in 2005 by

The People's History Ltd
Suite 1, Byron House
Seaham Grange Business Park, Seaham
County Durham SR7 0PY

ISBN: 1 902527 09 7

Contents

St MARY'S CHURCH ra BIT OF OLD GATESHEAD

Built in the 14th century and in use until the late 1970s St Mary's was the parish church of Gateshead. The authors believe that there was a church close to this site many centuries ago, but in 1080 it was burned down by locals with the Bishop of Durham inside. St Mary's has also suffered a major fire. Since then it has been used by the auctioneers Phillips and as a visitor information centre.

Introduction

This book contains over 200 images of Gateshead and the surrounding area. It was put together over three years and has grown and changed during that time. Originally this was to be a collection of old postcards drawn largely from Johnston's Monarch series, however, we also found a number of old photographs, and not quite so old photographs, that were worth including. With some we found that the areas they depicted had changed so radically over the years that gathering them together into a 'then and now' chapter was a good idea, with new images taken in the same place. Then production of the book slowed while change in Gateshead accelerated so some of the 'now' pictures even became out of date. The book was finally put together over the summer of 2005 with photographs being added almost to the end.

We would like to thank Andrew Clark for his patience and George Nairn for use of some of collection. We would also like to thank Jim, Julian and Justin at Beamish the North of England Open Air Museum photo archives for their help and the museum for use of some of the photographs. Some of the tramway photographs were supplied by the National Tramway Museum at Crich.

Special mention to Sarah Jane April Roddam

A parade of solders passes St Joseph's Church in 1906.

COME BIG STORE SHOPPING

As Gateshead's modernisation plans develop so too does Shephards ..... Gateshead's own major department store—the store that is ever looking to the future.

YOU'LL ENJOY SHOPPING AT SHEPHARDS

People travel to Shephards from all parts of Northumberland and Durham. This super store has its own car park, over 40 departments on four spacious floors, a delightful restaurant, a snack bar, Escalators to all upper floors ... and even a Barber's Shop! Everything for the home and family including fashions, furniture, footwear and accessories, fancy goods, linens, household appliances and carpets. The complete department store that's packed with exciting new ideas—*Come tomorrow!*

SHEPHARDS of GATESHEAD

WEST St. and ELLISON St., GATESHEAD.

An advert for one of Gateshead's most famous department stores from the 1960s.

AROUND GATESHEAD

CO-OPERATIVE STORES AND HALL, WHITEHALL ROAD, GATESHEAD 574

The Gateshead area has strong associations with the Co-operative movement. This postcard shows the store and hall in Whitehall Road.

Gateshead riverside has seen some remarkable changes over the last few years. Many old buildings have gone and its certainly arguable that much good has been demolished along with the bad. This postcard shows the Bottle Bank area, *circa* 1900.

The Gateshead premises of the National Provincial Bank. The first bank in Gateshead seems to have been opened in 1865. Later a branch of the North Eastern Bank opened at Central Buildings, High Street in 1873.

Town Hall. Gateshead.

Gateshead Town Hall. The building's exterior remains much the same today, however, the forecourt has changed and recent road reconstruction has altered the area greatly. The front of the building features a commemorative window to town hall clerks, Joseph Willis Swinburn and William Swinburn.

Some slightly lurid headlines are being displayed at this Anderson's Newsagents stall. The men pictured are believed to be Bill Anderson and Arthur Shepard. Gateshead's first newspaper, the Gateshead Observer, was founded by W.H. Brocket in 1837. It had a moderately reformist tone. It soon developed a high reputation for itself which declined under later ownership, ending its days in 1886 filled with accounts of scandal and disaster.

Greenesfield Locomotive Works. The site was originally a railway station. The works were established around 1852 shortly after the opening of the High Level Bridge. They employed around 200 men and by 1910 more than three thousand.

Right: Willie Hopper's 'The Golden Teapot' on the corner of John Street. Although close physically Gateshead and Newcastle are very different to each other. One area this is apparent is shopping. Newcastle has been able to support several department stores where Gateshead has often struggled to keep one. While the town has had and still has a number of thriving small shops many Gateshead folk seemed happy to cross the Tyne into Newcastle to make many of their purchases. In spite of over a century of attempts by Gateshead it has taken the establishment of the MetroCentre to redress the balance.

Below: Jackson Street with carnival decorations in the 1930s.

Gateshead Carnival, Jackson Street Decorations.

The shop in High Street West of R. Johnston & Sons who published the series of Monarch picture postcards – many of which are contained in this book. Monarch cards are something of a collector's item. In January 1946 a fire destroyed Johnston's shop and negatives and records all went up in flames.

The exterior of T. Waugh general dealers shop.

Shopping at Pelaw looking towards the CWS Works.

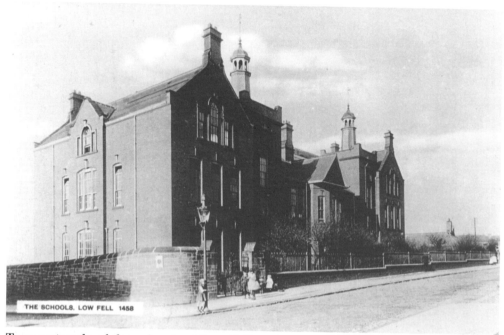

THE SCHOOLS, LOW FELL 1458

Two postcards of the schools at Low Fell and the Abbot Memorial School. As in many industrial areas education has often been motivated by religious groups and the needs of industry as well as the more liberal view that education is valuable for education's sake. After the passing of the Elementary Education Act of 1870 a census committee found that of over eight thousand children of school age only about half were receiving what could reasonably be described as an education. The Abbot School was built in 1869 by the widow of local industrialist John Abbot to help what were sometimes referred to as 'gutter children'. The school closed its doors in 1930 and was eventually demolished in 1968.

ABBOTT MEMORIAL SCHOOL, GATESHEAD

The New Bridge Inn. This public house is now the Metropole.

A 1930s view of Heworth and Pelaw in Johnston's Monarch series of picture postcards.

A Run on The Bank in Gateshead

In the early 1900s postcards could often feature topical events such as important weddings, the opening of buildings and the occasional accident. Several exist of local train crashes and other disasters. This image must have been an absolute gift to the contemporary caption writer.

Church Street, Blaydon, in 1903. A sign on the shop on the left declares: 'Ladies & Gents Boots & Shoes – Style & Quality Unequalled!'

Post Office & Morley Avenue, Bill Quay   8626

J. Welch's confectioner's, tobacconist's and post office in Morley Avenue at Bill Quay in the 1930s.

Although much has changed its still very easy to recognise this general view of Heworth.

Sodhouse Bank,
Sheriff Hill,
Gateshead.

Sodhouse Bank at Sheriff Hill in the early 1900s.

A rather traditional looking Co-operative Society shop at Pelaw. The window on the left seems to be displaying clothing while that on the right includes what seems to be children's toys.

Here modernity is creeping in. This is the Felling Shore, Heworth & Bill Quay Co-operative Society general food store. The date in the stone above the shop doorway shows 1930.

A 1920s postcard view of Felling High Street.

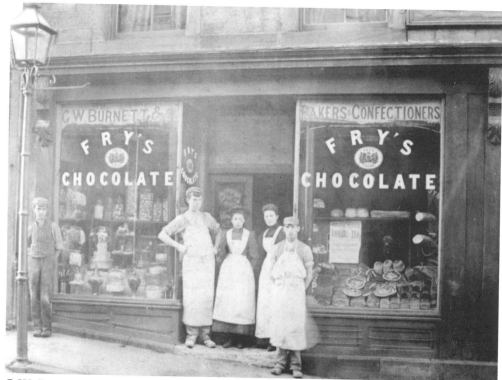

C.W. Burnet and Co, Bakers and Confectioners, Felling High Street. The staff pictured here all seem rather young. The boy to the far left looks isolated. Is he also a shop employee or did he just want to be in the picture?

Exeter Street – the view of this street today is remarkably similar.

A rather happy and busy view of Sunderland Road. As with the above postcard most of the children have paused for the photographer. It would be interesting to draw contrasts between the lives of the children featured.

Although this is likely to be a commissioned photograph, here the premises of Gateshead Industrial Co-operative Society certainly look very clean efficient and organised.

Heavy haulage by Pickford's outside the Ritz with the police on hand to control the traffic in the mid 1950s.

A rather pastoral view of Lobley Hill. However, the rather tranquil foreground is set against a background showing the endless progress of the industrial revolution. Behind the horse and carts are rows of houses and factories.

THE AVENUE. DUNSTON. (265)

Some of Gateshead's more distinctive buildings – The Avenue in Dunston.

Blaydon Burn, *circa* 1902.

Looking along Coatsworth Road. The horse still rules the road but the electric tram has arrived. The infant internal combustion engine would soon be on the scene.

Road works in Ravensworth Road, Dunston in the late 1920s showing road surfacing taking place. A horse and cart works alongside a steam roller.

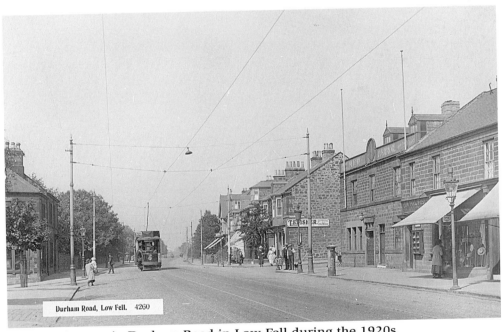

An electric tram in Durham Road in Low Fell during the 1920s.

You don't have to go back generations to see the changes in the face of Gateshead. This side of Wilkinson's store is now completely enclosed inside the new bus and Metro interchange.

THE CO-OPERATIVE WHOLESALE SOCIETY

Cover of *The Producer*, the Co-operative Wholesale Society magazine. The cover and the contents feature Pelaw Down Quilts.

A bird's eye view of the Pelaw works. Pelaw station is in the foreground. This is one of a series of rather nice illustrations of the factory.

The CWS works at Pelaw are often referred to in CWS literature as being at Newcastle. This is likely to be because the Newcastle branch committee seem to have originally intended to establish a factory in Newcastle but opted for Pelaw when they discovered a large area of land with good railway connections that could be obtained at a very small cost and that rates and taxes in this area would be much lower.

A Co-operative Society guide, *circa* 1914, proudly stated some facts and figures about the Pelaw works:

'The Clothing factory contained four departments. On the ground floor the kersey department manufactured miners' and artisans' clothing and also the tailoring department for the production of bespoke clothing. The top floor was devoted to the production of men's woollen shirts and ladies underclothing. The first floor contained the cutting room for tailoring shirts and underclothing and stockroom.

All machines are of the high speed type and electrically driven. The girls use patent adjustable seats, which add much to their comfort; the workrooms are light and airy, and labour is lightened by the use of machinery in every direction.

Wages are fixed by piece work, and also hour work, the rates being above the average in the district.

The Drug and Distillery Works has several specialities notably Pelaw Polish. Up to three hundred different articles are produced here at any one time.'

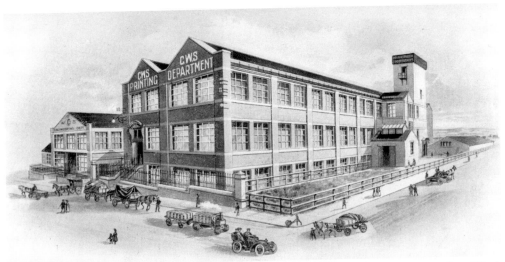

The printing works at Pelaw. The printing works originally commenced at West Blandford Street in the spring of 1898. In July 1902 the department moved to the new works at Pelaw where the paper and printing departments carried on jointly until June 1908 when development of the business meant the separation of the two departments. The walls inside were lined with white glazed bricks which made it easier to detect and clean away dirt. The rooms were all heated and ventilated by the Sirocco system with a powerful fan driving warm air into the building.

The factory from the opposite side. Pelaw station is behind. The cabinet factory was designed with the flow of work very much in mind. Railway wagons containing timber arrived at the back and were unloaded by travelling electric crane into the timber yard and store shed. The heat from the power house boilers helped dry the timbers. A system of exhaust pipes sucked the dust and shavings from the machines and deposited them into the boiler house.

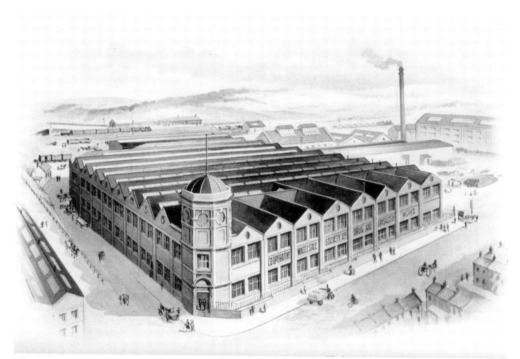

The CWS drug and drysaltery works. The area behind the building looks rather rural.

The CWS clothing factory.

The outside of the tailoring department.

Timber being unloaded at the factory's railway sidings. Pelaw station footbridge can be seen behind.

Box covering at the printing works. There would undoubtedly be a lot of noise which photographs often do not evoke. Seen in old photographs this looks a very clean and civilised scene compared with many other images of the time.

Letterpress bookbinding at the printing works.

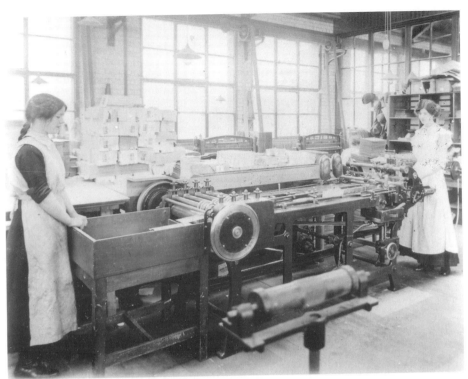

A carton gluing machine at the works.

The carton depot where the rigid boxes were made up and stapled.

Pelaw Down Quilts

The down quilts department had began as part of the cabinet factory but became a separate department in 1935. It was successful enough to prompt a virtual rebuilding of the factory in 1939 which was finished just after the outbreak of war. The department attracted the attention of the Ministry of Aircraft production and for the next four years played a vital part in the winning of the war in the air, producing electrically heated suits for high altitude flying. After the war the department went back to the production of down quilts although austerity governed what could be produced.

Joyce Carlson who worked at CWS Pelaw recalls: 'I started during the war in 1942 at the age of 14. On my first day I had to report to a designer called Mrs Smeaton. Their design studio had two large windows, lino on the floor, two large drawing desks, a wardrobe and a sliding glass bookcase. She had her desk and I had mine. She wasn't always an easy woman to work alongside. I had to tell her each time I went out of the office for something. The office staff had a separate canteen from the people who worked in

Cutter, Edna Knights, and designer, Joyce Wilkinson (Carlson) at work at the down quilts factory.

the factory. Ours was very nice. It had a table with a white cloth on. There was a waitress in a black dress with a white pinny and black cap with white lace on. Food rationing was on then and you had to work there for a year before you were allowed anything from the canteen with meat in it. I usually had a plate of chips and salmon cakes. Now and again if Dorothy Smeaton fancied salmon cake she would order a meat dish and we would swap.

In the canteen on Friday it was always fish and chips. One Friday when the fish arrived at our table it smelt off. So we sent it back. The manageress brought it back and said that we couldn't send it back because it was insulting to her. We refused to eat it and she insisted that we did. It all got out of hand and we were reported to Mr Swann, the manager of the quilt factory and were ordered into his office. We were told we had to apologise. Mr Swann passed the fish over to the under-manager, Stan Denton, and said you would eat that wouldn't you. Stan looked at it and said no he wouldn't. Mr Swann wasn't happy about that, the row started again, three of the girls handed their notice in and the rest of us never went back to the canteen.

I was a designer and designed quilts and bedspreads and pillowcases. Everything including the embroidery had to be drawn out full size on a white paper pattern. The factory had a government contract to make flying suits and jungle suits. We also made silk linings for flying boots. We had to spend a lot of time organising the patterns so as to waste as little material as possible.

Every year there was a show, the British Industrial Fair at Earls Court, and some of my work was exhibited there.

There was always a Christmas party. All of the staff would go to the rest room next to the showroom. The manger would be there and we would sit in a circle with a glass of sherry each making polite conversation. I was always glad when it was over. Then I could go and sit with other friends in the factory and have tea and cakes.

I left the works when I was twenty-six.'

Staff of CWS Pelaw down quilts factory. They are gathered together for a retirement presentation to Miss Handyside (with the flowers). The date is around 1953.

Two views of workers on the front lawn of the factory at Pelaw. Included are: Maureen Sinclair, Evelyn Black, Evelyn Stoves, Fred Screen and Norman George.

Material on the CWS Pelaw cutting bench with material destined to become swim and beach suits.

One of Pelaw's famous quilted down dressing gowns.

Another stage in the fashioning of swim and beach wear – overlocking on high speed machines.

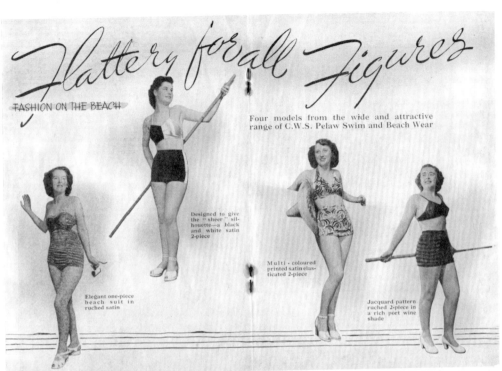

Flattery for all Figures

FASHION ON THE BEACH

Four models from the wide and attractive range of C.W.S. Pelaw Swim and Beach Wear

Designed to give the "sheer" silhouette—a black and white satin 2-piece

Multi-coloured printed satin elasticated 2-piece

Elegant one-piece beach suit in ruched satin

Jacquard pattern ruched 2-piece in a rich port wine shade

Swim and beach wear designed by Joyce Wilkinson (Carlson).

John Alnwick and Ken Horden in the stockroom at Pelaw down quilts in 1950.

The CWS flour works, Dunston. They opened on 18th April 1891. The flour milling machinery was situated in the building at the rear of this 1914 view. Wheat cleaning was undertaken in the building to the immediate right. The mills were divided into three distinct plants with a total output in 1914 of around 75 sacks of flour per hour. The grain silos could hold 15,000 tons of wheat which could be discharged directly into vessels alongside through powerful ship elevators. Three railway sidings allowed the loading of a thirty-five wagon train.

The CWS soap works, Dunston. The CWS originally intended to build the works on a stretch of ground at Pelaw, but fell back on the smaller Dunston site which was locked in by a road, a railway, a river and the CWS flour mill. The works basement was level with the river wharf. Liquids such as tallow were melted in the basement and pumped up to the pan room on the top floor while solid materials were taken up by lifts. During the production process the materials gradually descended to the ground floor which was level with trucks waiting for loading on a railway siding.

The flour mills at the CWS Dunston works.

A group of workers at the CWS works in Dunston. Electric cranes were used at the works to unload barrels of tallow and other materials.

FLOUR MILLS, DUNSTON. (505

A view of the CWS Dunston flour mills from the riverside, *circa* 1912.

NEW GRAIN ELEVATORS, C.W.S. WHARF, DUNSTON-ON-TYNE. (237)

New grain elevators at the CWS wharf at Dunston, also from around 1912.

TRANSPORT

1111. RAILWAY STATION, BLAYDON

A postcard of Blaydon railway station. The signal gantry dominates this image in a way that seems slightly unusual with the station and a train being little more than details. Did the photographer also opt to photograph the train moving under the gantry belching smoke and steam? This would be the more traditional railway image of speed and power. This picture was to be used in a then and now section. When getting to Blaydon we were able to reach the spot the picture had been taken. The platforms and the main tracks were still in place but just about everything else had gone. The view was also so obscured by vegetation that the photograph taken was not worth using.

Passengers changing from train to tram in Wellington Street. The entrance to the High Level Bridge is under and to the left of the camera. The tram seems to be at its terminus with the tracks not yet running across the High Level Bridge.

Wellington Street, Gateshead. 5905

In this later view the tracks are in position, motor buses have appeared but the crowds using public transport seem no less numerous.

The Northern Bus station at Wellington Street. Until the 1920s most motorbus services terminated in this area rather than cross the Tyne into Newcastle.

What seems to be major roadworks or road reconstruction underway in Wellington Street.

Above: Two early Gateshead and District Tramways electric cars at Wellington Street. Gateshead is unusual that although it had steam and electric tramways it never had a horse tram system. The Gateshead and District Tramways Company was formed in 1880 to construct three foot six inch tramways in the area. Horses were initially seen as the preferred motive power but realisation of the steep banks they would have to climb brought a change to steam power and also the gauge was increased to four foot eight and a half inches. Six miles of track covering three routes, to Heworth, Low Fell and The Teams were laid. *Below*: A Newcastle Corporation car in Wellington Street. Cross Tyne tram services began in 1923. (Photograph courtesy of the National Tramway Museum – taken by I.A. Yearsley, 9th August 1949.)

Wellington Street – photograph courtesy of the National Tramway Museum, taken by D.W.K. Jones, 1930. At this time the area would then have been a major transport interchange. The British Electric Traction Company had bought a controlling interest in the Gateshead lines in 1897. Two years later the Gateshead and District Tramways Act gave the company permission to electrify the existing routes and build others. Work started to convert the system to electric traction on 12th June 1900. The last steam tram ran 8th May 1901. The electric tram service was officially opened on the same day with a public service beginning the next day. The steam trams had been kept running as much as possible during construction. The large number of low bridges over the routes meant that many single deck cars were used on the system. Until 1904, when stopping places were introduced, car drivers could be hailed at any part of their routes. The Gateshead system was an undoubted success. In 1908 it was carrying twelve million passengers and paying shareholders a dividend of 7%. A pay as you enter system was tried, apparently the first on a British tramway, but was not an overall success. There was, however, much use of a penny universal fare.

Tramway crew in Wellington Street. They appear to be repairing a damaged trolley head. Picture courtesy of the National Tramway Museum – taken by D.W.K. Jones.

In the mid 1930s the option of replacing the trams with trolleybuses was considered by the company, but the corporation was also pursuing the option of compulsory purchase of the system and implementing their own trolleybus conversion plans. However, the war stopped both schemes. At the end of the Second World War the tram system was starting to show its age. Trolleybuses were again proposed by the company, they were already established in Newcastle, and the company may have desired to continue with the tradition of through running. However, in 1950 they obtained an Act of Parliament to convert to motor buses.

The last tram ran on 4th August 1951. The last car into the depot being No 16 which had been freshly painted for the occasion. Special souvenir tickets were printed and given out on the occasion. Several of the single deck cars were bought by British Railways and gave further service on their line at Grimsby. Unlike many other systems, the Gateshead trams, the last of the original electric trams on Tyneside, were able to retire with honour rather than the sad decline many systems suffered. Three of the single deck cars have been preserved. One, No 10, has given many years of service at Beamish Open Air Museum.

Above and below: Then and now views of Wellington Street. A street that was once a major transport interchange and the main thoroughfare for those crossing the Tyne has now lost its railway station and sees relatively little traffic. The arches have been home to a number of businesses and shops including the town's early Co-op.

Above and left: Gateshead Tramways staff. The group picture is likely to be shortly after the outbreak of the Second World War. The individual girl is likely to be from the time during the First World War. Gateshead Tramways staff seem to have had a very good reputation of always being friendly, more so than their Newcastle equivalents, and always turning out their tramcars in very good condition.

A tram on Gateshead High Street with the premises of Hedley & Co and
W. Younghusband on the right.

Tramcars at Heworth. The area to the left is now the site of Heworth bus and
Metro interchange.

One of the company's two axle open top double deck cars. It is interesting, given the British climate that so many tramway undertakings initially choose to order open topped cars. This seems to be partly a carry over from the days of the horse bus where the absence of a top cover meant less weight for the horse. However, in the early days of tramways, cars could run at a profit with only the saloon full and the top deck was seen as just extra revenue. Passenger complaints and rising costs gradually forced the top covering of most cars. Below one of the system's top covered cars.

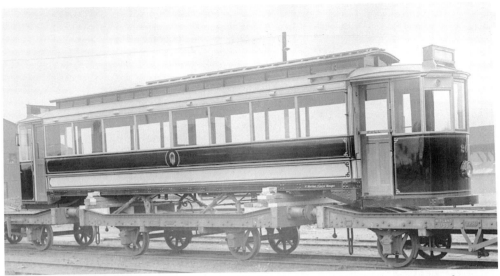

When in 1921 Gateshead Council decided not to exercise their option to buy out the tramway then the company decided to invest in modernising their fleet. A number of new trams were built while some of the old cars were rebuilt with more modern features. Above is pictured a body of a fully enclosed single deck car. The deployment of these cars must have come as a relief to many of the drivers. One of the cars is seen below towards the end of its life in Gateshead around 1950.

Management and crew pose with a car at the Sunderland Road car sheds. This is likely to be close to the system's opening. The sheds were of relatively lightweight construction when compared with what was built by corporations such as South Shields and Newcastle. Corporation depots where often built as status symbols. While private companies were prepared to spend money on improving the quality of their trams, depot buildings did little to generate profits and were built with an eye on economy. The depot site is today used as a Go Ahead bus depot although it is now difficult to detect any trace of the trams that were once there.

Gateshead was unusual in using so many single deck vehicles. This was due to a number of the lines running under low railway bridges. Here three staff members pose with one of the system's earlier four axle cars. Conductors seemed to have life easier than drivers. On cold days they spent at least some time moving around the warm interiors. Drivers spent all their time standing outside.

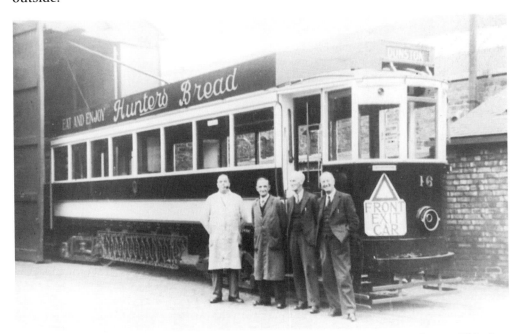

Gateshead and District Tramway staff with one of the cars at the depot. This is likely to be one of the last days of service.

Gateshead tram No 10 at Beamish. Three Gateshead trams have survived the scrap heap. After the Gateshead systems closure in 1951 No 10 along with several of its sisters was sold to British Railways to work on their Grimsby and Immingham railway. It remained there until that system's closure in July 1961. Number 10 has been a stalwart of the Beamish system being in service almost continuously since the museum's opening in 1973. Here popular television presenter James Burk is seen at the museum shooting a documentary.

An almost identical car is held by the National Tramway Museum. It is pictured at the museum's depot at Crich with Gateshead resident Babak Samsami. Another Gateshead car, a four wheeler, is held by the museum but is currently in storage.

Above: A Gateshead and District Tramway Company motorbus. The company had obtained the power to operate motor buses in 1909. In 1913 it began operating a feeder service from Chester-le-Street to the Low Fell tram terminus. The buses were apparently so successful at bringing in new business that the trams would fill up at the start of the journey into Gateshead and then speed past passengers waiting at tram stops. The motor buses were so profitable that the BET, Gateshead Tramways parent company registered the Northern General Transport Company on 29th November 1913. *Below*: The Tram and Omnibus waiting room at the Low Fell interchange in the 1920s.

Omnibus Station, Low Fell.   4288

The exterior and interior of a Northern bus. In the 1920s and '30s travelling across northern Durham in a solid tyred bus was hardly likely to be a comfortable experience. However, unlike the railways, buses actually ran into the centre of far flung towns and villages. Rail travel might have been more comfortable but getting on a bus probably meant less time was spent walking.

A locomotive and train at the platform of Swalwell station.

The Oldest Station in the World. Felling.

The first Felling station which opened on 5th September 1839 as part of the Brandling Junction railway. The main building is to the left, the waiting room to the right. It closed on 18th November 1896 to be replaced by a much larger island station consisting of a rather nondescript brick building, but with a rather large awning covering both platforms. This station remained well kept and lit by gas until around 1970. It was unstaffed from 1969 and suffered extensive vandalism. The buildings were demolished in 1972. The station closed for Metro construction work in 1979. The main building of the 1839 station is still standing.

THE RAILWAY STATION, DUNSTON-ON-TYNE. (230)

Two postcards of Gateshead railway stations from before the First World War – Dunston (*above*) and Swalwell (*below*). Gateshead seems to have had a difficult relationship with railway companies. There were contemporary observations that while companies were prepared to use Gateshead and its citizens to get their railways built, they did little to promote travel to Gateshead or advance communication inside it once the railways were in place. The companies were mainly interested in getting people, including Gateshead people, in and out of Newcastle which did little to develop shopping or commerce in the town.

RAILWAY STATION, SWALWELL. 1440.

N.E.R. FITTING SHOP, GATESHEAD.

Two views of the interior of Greenesfield locomotive works, *circa* 1907. The works were actually created out of the remains of Greenesfield station. This was the original terminus for direct trains from Tyneside to London. Once a great employer, the works declined then was revived and finally abandoned. There were proposals that the site become an annexe of the National Railway Museum. The site is now being redeveloped as luxury apartments, some of the works buildings have been incorporated into the new development but little of the original Greenesfield station remains.

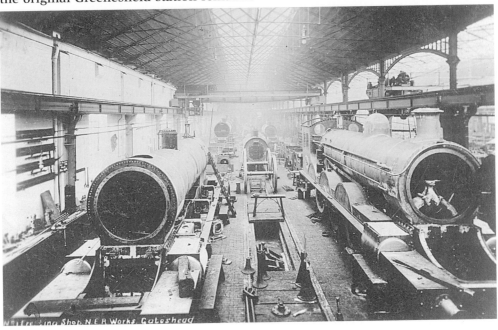

Erecting Shop, N E R Works, Gateshead

Locomotives outside Greenesfield works, *circa* 1980. The view was taken from a passing train. As mentioned the works were on the site of Greenesfield station. Although Newcastle Central Station and two cross Tyne railway bridges might now seem the logical arrangement for central Tyneside there were several vastly different alternatives proposed by competing railway interests before the present arrangement came into being.

'The Railway King' George Hudson had established a firm hold over the major North East rail routes. By the late 1830s the drive was on to inaugurate a direct service from London to the North East. Greenesfield station was opened on 15th January 1839. A ceremonial train made the journey from York to Gateshead in May 1844 and services between London Euston and Gateshead began a month later. It looked possible that Greenesfield would become the major Tyneside terminal station with Newcastle passengers crossing the Tyne by road. Scottish passengers also had to use the road crossing and it might have led to Newcastle and Gateshead becoming a stopover point for them. The station was quite a grand affair and included a refreshment area and small hotel. The designer was G.T. Andrews and was one of several fine stations he designed. A rail bridge crossing the Tyne was proposed but substantially further down the Tyne rather than between Newcastle and Gateshead.

What was to scupper this arrangement was the High Level Bridge. In 1845 Newcastle still did not have a proper railway station, but a number of temporary termini. Newcastle council and the Newcastle and Carlisle Railway wanted a unified station in Newcastle. Newcastle council were determined that the city would have Tyneside's major railway station. Although Hudson had Greenesfield station up and running he needed the support of the council and the Newcastle and Carlisle Railway for his proposed line for Berwick. A high level road bridge was also becoming a necessity to cross the Tyne and the two projects could be incorporated. A bargain seems to have been struck and Hudson began work on the High Level Bridge. This made a terminus in Gateshead superfluous and after the opening of the High Level Bridge the station closed to passengers. Greenesfield then became a locomotive works and by 1900 a major employer in the town.

After the opening of the High Level Bridge cross Tyne rail traffic expanded and it was obvious that the three tracks of the High Level Bridge were not enough to cope. There were proposals for another bridge but it took the North Eastern Railways some time to muster the necessary will and capital to begin construction. These photographs seem to show engineering and/or management staff visiting the site.

Above: A group of four men inside what would appear to be a small office used in the construction of the High Level Bridge. The photograph seems to be posed in order to provide a memorial to a fallen comrade. The empty chair being symbolic of his absence. On the deck there seems to be a model crane. *Below*: Construction work proceeding on the bridge.

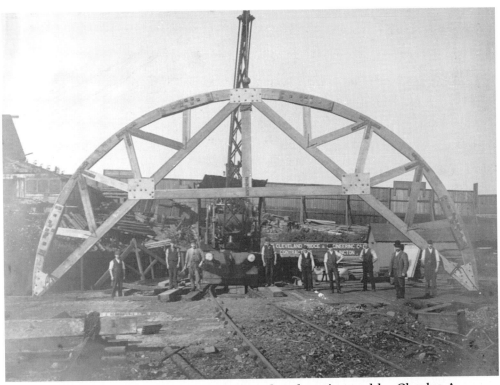

Above: Work on the bridge. It was designed and engineered by Charles A. Harrison, the Chief Civil Engineer of the North Eastern Railway. Slight embarrassment was caused to the NER by the need to demolish part of the recently constructed Forth Banks goods station to accommodate the approach tracks on the Newcastle side. *Below*: The approach road on the Newcastle side before the installation of the tracks.

Above: The bridge takes shape. The bridge was opened by King Edward VII and Queen Alexandra on 10th July 1906. It has a total length of 1,150 feet and was built by the Cleveland Bridge & Engineering Company. The foundation stone had been laid in July 1902. Building work took just over four years. *Below*: Banners for the opening of the bridge.

The High Level Bridge. Prior to the opening of the King Edward Bridge train movements across this were very intense and train weights are now far higher than the builders could have imagined. *Below*: Track renewal work taking place on the High Level Bridge. Recently the number of tracks on the bridge has been reduced to two. At the time of writing restoration work is taking place and there is talk of limiting traffic across it to help preserve it for future generations.

A view of the riverside from the Gateshead bank in 1890. The scene shows just how busy the Tyne was towards the end of the nineteenth century. The gorge between Newcastle and Gateshead is a natural barrier to communication. The first Newcastle/Gateshead bridge in the area is credited to the Romans. It was destroyed in 1248 and replaced by the Bishop of Durham in 1250. This was destroyed by a flood in 1771. A new bridge was in place by 1781 which was itself replaced by the swing bridge in 1876. A high level bridge had been proposed in 1771, but those with interests vested in the existing bridge and the roads around Newcastle and Gateshead quayside were successful in resisting it.

A horse bus service operated across the High Level Bridge for many years. The fair was a half penny, up to forty passengers were carried in a single carriage. Although convenient for many passengers this service dose not seem to have had a very high reputation and over the years there were charges of animal cruelty. The service seems to have been a thorn in the side of other local transport operators including the North Eastern Railway who owned the bridge. Tram operations began across the High Level Bridge in 1923 and across the Tyne Bridge in 1928. Around 1840 many people in Gateshead saw the building of better cross Tyne links as a good way of attracting the population of Newcastle into Gateshead both to shop and enjoy recreation and public holidays. However as the links were built they seem to have had the reverse effect with more people from Gateshead using them to get to Newcastle than vice versa.

The High Level Bridge viewed from Gateshead. The bridge would have provided some spectacular new views of the Tyne to the general public. However, only years after its opening it became a grandstand for one of then most spectacular sights in Tyneside's history – the explosion during the Great Fire of Gateshead and Newcastle of 1854. The fire started on the morning of Friday 6th October 1854. This account is largely drawn from a contemporary record. On the morning between twelve and one o'clock, a fire broke out in the worsted manufactory of Messrs Wilson and Sons, in Hillgate, Gateshead. After about two hours the roof fell in, and the heat became so intense it melted the sulphur stored in an adjoining bonded warehouse. It came out in torrents, like streams of lava; and, as it met the external air, began to blaze – its combustion illuminating the river and its shipping, the Tyne and the High Level Bridge in a lurid and purple light. The flames towered far above the masts of the ships

moored at the neighbouring quays. In the immediate neighbourhood was another bonded warehouse, filled with the most combustible materials – naptha, nitrate of soda, and potash, as well as immense quantities of tallow and sulphur; it is also said that a large quantity of gunpowder was contained in it. Those watching the fires seem to have known what was in the building and what would happen if the heat reached inside. Suddenly there was a huge devastating explosion which made Newcastle and Gateshead shake to their foundations. The sight was best witnessed from the High Level Bridge, which was crowded at the moment with anxious spectators. The bridge shook as if it would fall to pieces. That triumph of engineering skill began to vibrate like a piece of thin wire, and the first thought of those upon it was, that magnificent erection was about to fall. The projection of the flaming materials across the river was a wonderful sight for those who had coolness enough to witness it, but there were very few in that condition. A universal stupor seems rather to have prevailed everywhere, first broken by the screams and wailings of women and children, and by the ignition of the houses on the Newcastle side of the river. It was some time, however, before the minds of the spectators awoke to the full extent of the calamity. Broken glass was under your foot at every step. The shock of the tremendous explosion was felt over the whole eastern seaboard, from Blyth, in Northumberland, to Seaham, six miles to the south of Sunderland. In the streets in the neighbourhood of the explosion men, women, and children in their night dresses might be seen rushing from their abodes in search of shelter. In Gateshead particularly the scene was most distressing – mothers were vainly trying to return for a child, forgotten in the suddenness of escape – and children were searching for their parents. The tenements of the poor who lived in the vicinity of the warehouses, fell like houses built of cards, and, in some cases, it is said, buried their inmates in the ruins. All the houses in Church Walk, and Cannon Street, Gateshead, have been either partially or wholly destroyed, amounting to nearly fifty. Mr Craster, of the Gateshead Dispensary, was called to upwards of 100 cases, and most of the surgeons in Newcastle and Gateshead were attending sufferers at their own houses. The interior of St Mary's Church, Gateshead, is a ruin. Many of the grave-stones in the churchyard were removed by the force of the explosion, and thrown to a considerable distance, knocking in the walls of some of the adjoining houses. There was scarcely a house, office, or public building, within a radius of a hundred yards of the explosion, which had not been injured – either unroofed, or its windows broken. In Gateshead, the entire mass of buildings – extending several hundred yards – from Bridge Street and Church Street, eastward, and from Church Walk to the river, was entirely consumed. Church Walk was hardly passable; and Hillgate was completely choked up with the ruins.

An illustration showing fire fighters tackling the Great Fire of Gateshead. Men of Shields and Sunderland fire brigades rushed to help the local firemen. Some Tynesiders thought the Russian Navy had slipped up the river and bombarded the town (Britain was fighting the Russians in the Crimean War at this time).

A driver and delivery van from the Blaydon Co-op. Shopping at the Co-op or 'Store' was once an institution in North East communities. Shops such as the Blaydon Co-op provided for all the needs of Gateshead families. The motto of the Co-operative movement motto was: 'From the cradle to the grave' and their stores sold everything from baby clothes to funeral services. The Co-op also had the added attraction of providing a regular dividend ('divi'). Some families even used the 'divi' to pay for such occasions as weddings – with all the catering provided by the Co-op of course!

Felling Colliery. This is the downcast shaft. The coal chutes are on the immediate right. To the extreme left of the winding house is the lamp cabin. The shed on the right was the tub repair shop and was also used by surface workers as a bait cabin. Some of the former colliery buildings remain and part of the site is used for the sale of cars and car parts.

Above: Miners' pose for the photographer on the steps of the Fanny Pit. This was one of the three shafts at Heworth Colliery – the others were the John and Ada shafts. Mining first started in Heworth in the 1750s. The three shafts were sunk in the nineteenth century. The colliery's coal was shipped from the nearby Tyne staithes at Pelaw.

Left: A view of Heworth Colliery, *circa* 1917. The pit closed in 1963.

The conveyer screens at the Fanny Pit, Heworth, where coal was picked and sorted.

The conversion of London underground routes from steam to electric power resulted in many of the steam locos going on the second hand market and ending up in industrial settings. One is pictured here at Pelaw.

Two views of Pelaw Main Staithes at Bill Quay. The construction of a new steel chute seems to be in progress. The *SNA 7* (Navel Auxiliary) is tied to the staithes.

Above: The colliers *Krysanthis Patenas* and *Thirley* being loaded at Pelaw Main Staithes. *Below*: A view showing the cable hauled incline and three coal chutes. The staithes were unusual in that in the 1930s the spouts were replaced by wagon tippers.

The Norwood Pit at Dunston before the First World War.

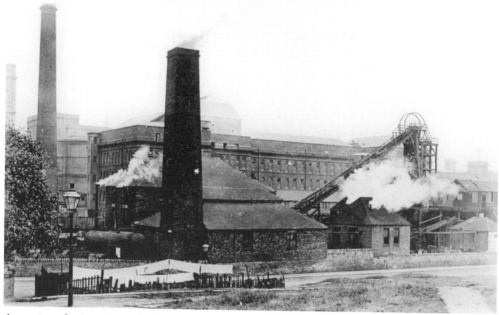

A postcard view from before the First World War of Dunston Colliery with the Co-operative flour mills behind.

A busy river scene showing ships loading coal at Dunston staithes in the years between the two world wars.

Rail and river transport side by side on the Tyne at Blaydon, *circa* 1920. A paddle boat steams up the river while rail tracks line the bank.

Workshops at Axwell Colliery in Swalwell. The first shaft was sunk in 1835.

A group of pit deputies at Axwell Park Colliery.

Ravensworth Lodge Banner with band and officials.

Workers at Springwell quarry. Many of these former stone quarries have since been redeveloped and landscaped as recreational areas.

Workers posing beside a lorry in a gas works. The Newcastle and Gateshead
Gas Company was founded in 1817. By 1911 it was supplying gas to Newcastle,
Gateshead, Dunston, Blaydon, Newburn, Felling and several adjacent areas. At
that time gas was selling for 2s and 2d per 1000 cubic feet with discounts of up
to 25% for prompt payment. Gas works were situated at Elswick and at
Redheugh. To cope with peaks in demand the Redheugh works was equipped
with an oil gas-plant which could be brought into use at a few hours notice.

A Gateshead Corporation lorry apparently used for transporting Pulverised
Manure.

The premises of the United Alkali Co Ltd Allhusen works at Gateshead.

Felling Chemical Works Disaster

The *Monthly Chronicle* reported a chemical works explosion on 26th July 1891.

An appalling catastrophe occurred at the Friar's Goose Chemical Works, near Gateshead. Shortly before seven o'clock in the evening, when the night-shift men had gone in to duty, four of the condensers suddenly collapsed, burying the following seven workmen in the ruins:– William Parkinson, aged 25; George Robertson, 47; William Heslop, 40; James McCuskin, 50; James McTierman, 52; Henry Shorey, 45; and Robert Johnson, 50. The whole of these were instantly killed, with the exception of McCuskin, who was held fast between two great slabs of stone, which imprisoned him tightly without crushing him. The most strenuous efforts were put forth with a view of rescuing him from his perilous position, but, unhappily, without success, as the poor fellow, after bearing his sufferings most manfully and heroically for twelve hours, at last exclaimed 'I'm done,' and expired. The whole of the seven men who met with so sad a fate were married, except Parkinson. As to the cause of the accident, it was stated that the water had been turned on to the tank, for the purpose of extinguishing the fire which had caught the coke in one of the condensing chambers below. Steam was thereby quickly generated, and, not finding ready vent, was sufficient to cause an explosion. This brought the centre condenser down, and, the whole framework being loosened, the others followed.

Left: Two men whose trade was apparently bleachpacking, the cloths around their faces presumably being some attempt at heath protection.

Below: An illustration showing the premises of Messes Hoyle, Robson, Barnett and Co. The company was established in 1798.

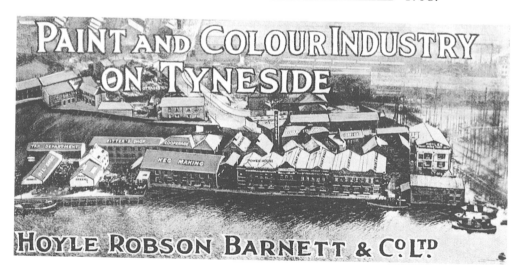

PAINT AND COLOUR INDUSTRY ON TYNESIDE

HOYLE ROBSON BARNETT & CO LTD

Above: Part of a laboratory at Hoyle, Robson, Barnett and Co. The company 'struck' colours such as chromes, reds and blues, Prussian, Brunswick and fast reds and reflex blues and also Chinese and Persian led reds. They were proud of their black department which produced blacks in all forms – pulp, powdered, drop or cake and paint. A system using waste steam was designed to dry the colours.

Left: The mixing of paint, partly assisted by gravity, was carried out over three floors.

Construction work on Dunston Power station. This was one of the most advanced power stations in the world in the 1930s. Hoppers full of ash from the station could be seen being towed down the Tyne for dumping out at sea. An extension was built after the Second World War. At one point the station occupied an area of approximately 75 acres and had a river frontage of about a quarter of a mile. The power station ran until the 1970s. After closure some of the site was used for part of the MetroCentre.

Work approaching completion on Dunston power station.

The gatehouse to the abandoned and forlorn Dunston power station. The picture was taken around 1981. At this time much of the surrounding area was awaiting redevelopment into Gateshead MetroCentre.

A view overlooking Felling Colliery down to the Tyne and Bill Quay.

Dunston Coke Works. After closure and demolition the land was reclaimed as part of the 1990 National Garden Festival at Gateshead, many tons of contaminated soil and debris having to be scooped out and removed from the site. At the end of the festival much of the area was then developed as a housing estate.

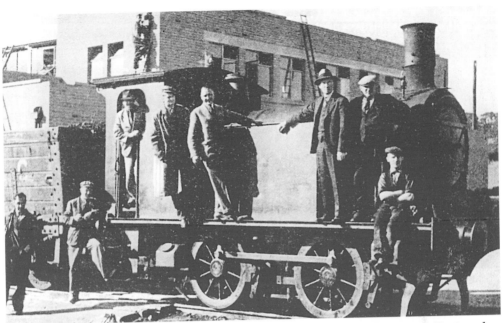

The 1930s saw some considerable economic depression in the North East and banks were not keen to lend money to companies to invest in the area. A previously uninvolved central government seems to have been galvanised by a General Election and the idea of government-sponsored trading estates was adopted. Huge yellow lorries appeared in the Team Valley levelling out the colliery spoil heaps for construction of the first estate. *Above*: An industrial locomotive employed on the site. *Below*: A North Eastern Railway crane locomotive from Greenesfield shed.

Above: The premises of W. R. Worley carriage maker of Low fell. *Below*: What appears to be the Gateshead premises of a track maker. This junction is likely to be part of as colliery internal railway and may have been located below ground. Junctions would often be laid out in the manufacturer's own yard to check all the parts actually fitted.

William Park, Brompton Street, Shoeing Forge.

A horse drawn mobile shop belonging to C.W. Burnett and Co, High Felling.
Their High Felling premises appear on page 20.

Cumberland or Middle White pigs at a farm in the Heworth area.

A horse and float ready for a show. The rolley (dray) belonged to G.W. Amos of South Farm, Wardley.

Richard Amos on a Ferguson tractor and John Amos beside a pair of horses. The occasion was a ploughing match at Wardley.

Men and horses ready for ploughing day in the Wardley area.

Life on a farm in the Wardley area, *circa* 1930. The girl is believed to be Sally Younger.

IN OUR SPARE TIME

Carnivals and parades have been a strong feature of life in Gateshead. This image shows local people onboard the Gateshead Express. This locomotive and coach seems to have been built out of a tractor and farm cart.

A view of Saltwell Wesleyan Chapel. The chapel was located on the corner of Rawlivery Road and Faraday Grove.

A group from Gateshead on a social outing.

THE LAKE. SALTWELL PARK, GATESHEAD

A view of the lake at Saltwell Park in the early 1900s. The council purchased land from William Wailes in 1875. A ground plan for the park was prepared by Edward Kemp. The park opened in 1876 and was extended in 1920.

Children and adults around the park boating lake.

Promenades are usually associated with the seaside but here ladies and children are seen relaxing along the promenade at Saltwell Park.

Three girls in front of the tea hut at Saltwell Park. This was a postcard sent to Tweedmouth in 1906.

Children in the playground at Gateshead Park.

rk.

Members of the Gateshead yacht club.

Children pose for the camera during a celebration in Gateshead.

A group of men outside the Crown Hotel. This is likely to be a 'works outing' of some kind. The man towards the middle may be the works proprietor, while the men in bowler hats may be foremen or some kind of supervisors. Those in the flat caps are of course the workers.

The West End Working Men's Club at Dunston.

The Lord Bishop of Durham DEDICATING THE GATESHEAD WAR MEMORIAL, 14th May 1922.

LOW FELL POST OF

T.S.PARKINSON B

Above: A postcard showing the Lord Bishop of Durham dedicating Gateshead War Memorial on 14th May 1922. In the 1920s memorials were built all over the country to remember the hundreds of thousands of men who had died in the First World War. Crowds flocked to witness their unveiling and to mourn those who did not return home.

Left: The War Memorial at Low Fell. This statue was erected in 1903 to the memory of men who had fallen in the 'South African Campaign' – better known as the Boer War.

There is a large gathering of people outside of Trinity Church for this postcard produced by Johnston of Gateshead. Was there a particular reason why they were here or are they just posing for the photographer?

A children's carnival in the 1920s. They are on the back of a lorry belonging to W. Goldthorp – joiner and builder – Park Terrace, Gateshead.

Two Women's Voluntary Services mobile canteens at Ashfield House, Joicey Road, Low Fell during the Second World War. The plaque on the top vehicle reads 'Presented by the American Red Cross in memory of Percy Chubb. A friend of Britain.' The inscription on the bottom vehicle reads 'Presented by the Uptown Branch Greater Boston Committee of the American Red Cross.'

GATESHEAD FOOTBALL CLUB

Above: Gateshead FC in the 1930s.

In 1930 Third Division North side South Shields moved lock stock and barrel to Gateshead. For the new 1930-31 season Gateshead took their place in the League with Redheugh Park hosting teams like Hull City, Wrexham and Carlisle United. In 1938 the club again stunned the football world with the signing of the great Hughie Gallacher. On his debut at Redheugh he scored five goals in a 7-1 victory over Rotherham United.

Gateshead finished third from bottom of the Fourth Division at the end of the 1959-60 season yet it was the Tynesiders who were voted out of the League.

Today Gateshead play in the Unibond Premier League and play their home games at the International Stadium.

Right: A programme from Gateshead's last season in the Football League.

GATESHEAD A.F.C. Ltd.

Division IV   Saturday, November 28th, 1959

GATESHEAD v WATFORD

Official Programme   *Season*
3d.   1959-60

INSIST ON THE BEST

HOGGETT'S FAMOUS PRODUCTS
(Est. 1924)

BEETROOT

PICKLED ONIONS   RED CABBAGE
PICCALILLI   VINHOGG   POMPY SAUCE
MIXED PICKLE   TOMATO KETCHUP
SILVERSKINS   MALT VINEGAR   SWEET PICKLE

Hoggett's Potato Crisps still sell at 3d. per packet

HOGGETT'S FOOD PRODUCTS LTD.
NEW MODEL FACTORY,   ASKEW ROAD WEST,   GATESHEAD
Telephone: 7-1860

In 1981 Whickham reached the FA Challenge Vase Final at Wembley Stadium. Around 5,000 supporters travelled down from Whickham for the big day. Their opponents, Willenhall Town, got off to a flying start scoring two goals in the first ten minutes. However, goals from Scott and Williamson took the match into extra time. A shot from Billy Cawthra was deflected by a Willenhall defender into his own goal to give Whickham a famous victory.

Whickham Football Club was formed in 1944 and for a time were known as Axwell Park Colliery Welfare before returning to the name of Whickham in the early 1960s. When they reached the Vase Final in 1981 Whickham were a Wearside League side. The team now plays in the Northern League Division Two.

The victorious Whickham players coming down the steps from the Royal Box after receiving the FA Challenge Vase from the legendary Manchester United manager Sir Matt Busby.

Whickham players and officials with the FA Vase on the Wembley pitch on 25th April 1981.

The Whickham squad and back room staff in 1983-84 season. During this season Whickham reached the semi-final of the FA Vase but were knocked out by the eventual winners Stansted. Back row, left to right: Tommy Robinson (manager), Ian Diamond, Billy Riley, Peter Guthrie, Paul Heron, Geoffrey Mayne, Allan Young, Wilfred Keilty, David Farrey, Colin Telford. Front row: Malcolm Barkess (coach), Alan Barker, William Rafferty, Keith Knox, Derek Ward, Michael Spellman and John Hogg.

Gateshead International Stadium is one of the top sports arenas in the country today. The stadium celebrated its 50th anniversary on the August Bank Holiday weekend 2005. The stadium was opened by marathon runner Jim Peters on 27th August 1955.

The original Gateshead Youth Stadium had a cinder running track and asphalt cycle velodrome. In the 1970s the installation of the 'tartan' synthetic running track meant the old cycle track had to go.

Men like the late Stan Long worked tirelessly to build Gateshead Harriers into one of the top athletic clubs in the country.

The appointment of Brendan Foster as manager of Sports and Recreation at Gateshead Metropolitan Council as well as the improvements to the stadium was to put Gateshead on the map in terms of world athletics.

The inaugural meeting of the refurbished track on 3rd August 1974 could not have got off to a better start with a world record. The crowd at the first meeting saw Brendan Foster crown the occasion by setting a new world best for the 3,000 metres.

Left: Brendan Foster during his running days. Today he is one of the most well known faces on BBC television and is the man behind the Great North Run.

Youngsters enjoying the facilities of Gateshead International Stadium in September 2005.

Athletics is just one of the sports that the stadium plays host to today. Gateshead Football Club and Gateshead Thunder Rugby League Club play their home games at the stadium. As well as the main stadium there are a number of indoor facilities. Netball, basketball, tennis, football badminton, volleyball and boxing are just a some of the sports staged in the training hall. Other activities such as exhibitions and antique fairs are also held at Gateshead and the stadium can hold 38,000 for pop concerts.

Gateshead and Newcastle seem to both now offer much more in the way of entertainment to younger people. In the background can be seen the Tuxedo Princess, the famous floating nightclub.

This huge carousel wheel was erected on the Gateshead quayside during the visit of the tall ships to the Tyne in 2005.

EVER CHANGING VIEW

Construction underway on the Sage Music Centre. Much of the riverside area has seen huge changes over the past five years with the conversion of the Baltic flour mills into an art gallery, the construction of the Millennium Bridge, riverside flats and the Sage centre.

The area around St Mary's Church from the High Level Bridge. This is before the construction of the Tyne Bridge.

Construction underway on the Tyne Bridge. Note how the cards refers to it as the New High Level Bridge.

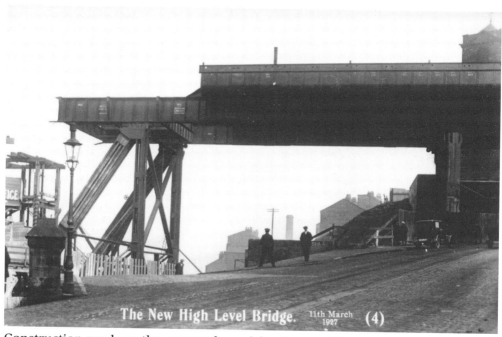

The New High Level Bridge. 11th March 1927 (4)

Construction work on the approach road for the new Tyne Bridge.

The need for a new Tyne bridge had been identified in Victorian times. However, it took until 1924 for firm proposals to take shape and work itself began in August 1925.

There are many photographs showing the two great arches of the bridge taking shape in a mass of cables and cranes. Men worked in what would now be considered appalling safety conditions with little or nothing in the way of safety harnesses or ropes about eighty feet over the water. Only one worker was killed during the construction of the bridge – Nathanial Collins, a scaffold erector. He fell over a hundred feet into the water and fractured his skull.

Work on the bridge was to take three years to complete. The bridge was built by Dorman and Long of Middlesbrough. The Tyne Bridge was designed by Mott, Hay and Anderson who based their design on the Sydney Harbour Bridge which was in turn derived from the Hell Gate Bridge in New York. Construction on the Australian contemporary was begun before the Newcastle one, however, the Sydney Harbour Bridge was not completed until 1932.

Several buildings were demolished to make way for the bridge including four pubs, a powder mill, a pickle factory and a bank.

The bridge's Cornish granite towers are not integral to the structures support. They were originally grain storage warehouses and lifts to give access to and from the quaysides. The original colour of the bridge was green but it has had many variations since.

High Street looking towards the future site of the Tyne Bridge.

Here the camera is in roughly the same place but the view is completely different. This image was taken mid 2004.

COOPERATIVE WHOLESALE SOCIETYS WORK PELAW

Although taken separately this photograph and the one of Pelaw station on the page opposite almost make up a panoramic view of the works and railway. The images below show how things have changed. The CWS factory has gone to be replaced by housing and a supermarket. The goods yard has closed although some of the buildings remain, now serving other uses. Goods trains are much less frequent and passenger trains have mostly given way to the Metro. Pelaw Station was opened in November 1896 and this was Pelaw's third station. Like Felling this was an island station accessed via a footbridge

although here the platform seems to have been wider, possibly because it is was a junction station. Pelaw became unstaffed in October 1965 and the building was demolished in 1972 to be replaced by a brick shelter. It closed in November 1979. Although completely demolished during Metro construction, the new tracks still curved around the space previously occupied by the platform. After the opening of the Metro the station was rebuilt – opening in September 1985. With the opening of the Sunderland Metro line Pelaw again became a junction station.

Road works taking place in the Gateshead area. The photograph above shows the men hard at work under the watchful eye of the two men on the right. However, in the picture below there seems to be no work taking place while the photographer's camera has produced a crowd of women and children.

Two views of Dunston – one old one new. This area used to be surrounded by industry, now it has been much reduced. The area has also seen much landscaping and the 1990 National Garden Festival was staged here.

Many of the old buildings in the Bottle Bank area were swept away by the building of the Tyne Bridge approach roads in the 1920s although some lingered on till around the turn of this century. However, almost all that was left has finally been demolished with the construction of the Hilton Hotel at Gateshead.

Construction work underway on the Hilton Hotel.

Looking up the High Street towards Durham Road in 2003.

A group of international students from the City of Sunderland College. As with Newcastle, often described as a party city, there are now many more reasons for people to travel to Gateshead for leisure rather than work.

The Tyne Metro bridge. Several initial plans of the Tyne and Wear Metro system did not envisage the Metro actually crossing the river. The need for this bridge and the line to Gateshead and South Shields was at one time in doubt. However, construction took place between 1976 and 1979. It was designed by Fairhurst and Partners and built by Cleveland Bridge & Engineering Co Ltd. The design is apparently based on the Ballachulish Bridge crossing the mouth of Loch Leven in Scotland. It is a through-truss steel girder construction and was built by simultaneous cantilever from each bank until the two sections met in

the middle in August 1978. It was opened by Queen Elizabeth II in November 1981. The total cost was over £6 million. If the Metro were to be built today its unlikely an independent bridge like this could be afforded.

The Gateshead entrance to the High Level Bridge in 2003. Construction is underway on the Hilton Hotel which will come to dominate much of this part of Gateshead. The overalled figures just visible on the bridge are involved in track replacement work.

Although long closed some of the structures from the former Felling Colliery still remain on the site. Around 1982 the area was used for the sale of second hand cars and car parts.

As soon as it was erected in 1998 the Angel of the North became one of the area's most famous landmarks. Its position alongside the A1 ensures 90,000 drivers a day get a fleeting view of the giant statue.

The celebrated artist Antony Gormley designed the 65 feet (20 metres) high steel structure. The wing span of 175 feet (54 metres) is the same as a modern day passenger aircraft.

The Arts Council Lottery Fund awarded £585,000 towards the cost of the Angel. Other contributors included the European Regional Development Fund, Northern Arts as well as private sponsors.

Hartlepool Steel Fabrication built the Angel with the help of consulting engineers Ove Arup and Partners and Gateshead Council.

The £70 million Sage Gateshead music centre was officially opened by the Queen on 14th October 2005. The Royal occasion had been postponed for six months because of the General Election.

The Queen and the Duke of Edinburgh were welcomed by Anthony Sargent the general director of the centre. Mr Sargent said 'After the original opening, where we basically threw open the doors to the community, we wanted a ceremonial opening that could add to that.'

Gateshead's multi-storey car park found fame in the movie world as one of the locations in *Get Carter*. Since its release in the early 1970s the film has gone on to become a cult classic.

In the film the character played by Michael Caine threw Cliff Brumby (played by Bryan Mosley) from the top of the car park.

When there was first talk of pulling down the car park the Get Carter Appreciation Society were one of those who called for the 1960s building to be saved.

The society's founder, Chris Riley, defends what has been described by some as brutalist architecture. 'It is a really iconic 1960s building. If you look across the Tyne from Newcastle city centre it dominates the skyline.'

BALTIC

FLOUR MILLS

GATESHEAD

This modern plant is a recent addition to the great milling enterprise of

JOSEPH RANK LIMITED

From here come vast quantities of high quality flours of many grades and also the famous Blue Cross balanced feeding-stuffs for livestock. Unceasing research ensures that the products of these mills are always in the forefront of dietetic progress for both man and his animals.

Joseph Rank Ltd

FLOUR MILLERS AND MANUFACTURERS OF ANIMAL FEEDING STUFFS

An advertisement for the Baltic Flour Mills from the early 1960s.

The Millennium Bridge being lowered into position on Monday 20th November 2000 by the Asian Hercules crane. When the bridge was proposed it generated some controversy with concerns, among others that navy ships would not be able to tie up at Newcastle, breaking centuries of tradition, and that it would see little use as it was 'a bridge to nowhere.' However, commissioning went ahead and the bridge was constructed in the AMEC yard at Wallsend. It is the most easterly bridge across the Tyne. It opened to the public in September 2001.

The completed Millennium Bridge with its famous neighbour – the Tyne Bridge.

Work in progress converting the old flour mill into an arts centre.

The Baltic in 2003. On the side of the building are banners advertising the work of Antony Gormley – the designer of the Angel of the North.

A temporary ice rink near the Millennium Bridge – a scene slightly
reminiscent of old postcards showing skaters on frozen over boating lakes.